THE MANAGER'S POCKET GUIDE TO

Workplace Coaching

by Daniel A. Feldman, Ph.D.

HRD PRESS
Amherst, Massachusetts

Published by:
HRD Press
22 Amherst Road
1-800-822-2801
(U.S. and Canada)
1-413-253-3488
1-413-253-3490 (Fax)
www.hrdpress.com

ISBN 0-87425-634-8

Cover design by Eileen Klockars
Production services by Anctil Virtual Office
Editorial services by Sally M. Farnham

Acknowledgments

I wish to thank my family, in particular my wife, Jo, for help and support throughout all aspects of this project. Thanks to my friend and colleague Jeff Kelly, who provided keen insights and suggestions. And many thanks to all the coaches I have had throughout my life, most importantly Gurumayi for the greatest teaching of all, believing in the power that lies within the human heart.

TABLE OF CONTENTS

Introduction

This book is designed to help mangers become better managers. When people are elevated to a management position, it is usually because they have done well at mastering the prerequisite technical skills. While knowledge of the technical side of the job is important, it doesn't provide guidance for how to be effective at managing people.

This book will help you to:

❖ Recognize the importance of assuming the role of coach while managing subordinate personnel.

❖ Approach your role of coach in the optimal way.

❖ Learn the key elements of the coaching process.

❖ Develop the different skills that foster good coaching communication.

❖ Identify the many forums available for coaching employees.

SECTION I
THE MANAGER AS COACH

Coaching in the Workplace

To begin our exploration of workplace coaching, let's first identify what you *don't* want in a coach. . . .

Eric Hampton had been at his new job as a marketing specialist for five months. He liked his job and his colleagues. During this period he had received no formal evaluation of his performance except for a couple of e-mails from his boss stating he was doing "a great job." He was finally scheduled to receive his three-month performance review, two months late.

He sat down with a representative from Human Resources prior to meeting with his immediate supervisor. The HR person said, "You might want to take some time to look over your performance review. Now don't be too upset; it's all to help you improve on your job."

Eric did get upset. The review was filled with negative feedback, much of which he didn't agree with, and only one vague statement about how, overall, he was doing OK on the job. He felt completely blindsided. When his boss came in, he said Eric wasn't doing things on time and made too many mistakes in his work.

His boss didn't suggest any detailed methods for improvement, commenting only that he thought "Eric could do better." The next day, Eric started looking for a new position.

What was missing in this scenario? What was the main reason for the employee leaving, creating extra hiring and training costs and loss of productivity?

Eric's boss didn't know how to be a coach!

What is coaching in the workplace? Coaching is acting in a way that promotes the continual development of the skills of the people in your organization. Why is coaching important? Because coaching can directly affect the bottom line of any organization. It is a critical tool for increasing productivity.

Coaching is . . .

acting in a way that promotes the continual development of the skills of the people in your organization.

More and more organizations are recognizing the importance of leadership for building a high-performing organization. Workplace leadership is about influencing people to perform at their highest level in achieving the goals of the organization. Coaching is the application of workplace leadership in the area of employee development.

To learn any skill fully, you need a guide. To learn how to handle a car safely, you need a driving teacher. To learn mathematics, you need a math teacher. The same goes for work. To get the most out of your work potential, a workplace coach can be invaluable.

Coaching is more than just showing someone the basic elements of a job. It's about guiding people to learn the most effective way of performing their job. Coaching opens up a person's perspective. Ideally, coaching expands the effectiveness of the employee, thus it helps the organization succeed.

➡ Case Example

The story of Nancy Green serves as a good case example for developing a coaching perspective. Nancy was the Branch Manager in a highly pressured sales office of a large computer company. Her sales people did most of their work over the phone.

Nancy was a strong decision maker who was very goal oriented and driven to succeed. She was a prodigious performer, doing the work of three people. She would often become a micromanager in the details of her subordinates' work. She had a communication style that, at times, was sharp and abrasive. She didn't have a problem with her top performers, or they with her. But she had lots of difficulties with other members of the staff who found her critical, pushy, and overbearing.

Nancy labeled her employees as "A performers" or "B performers." She thought that anyone who was not as motivated and driven as she, was a slacker. And her attitude showed in her communication with these employees.

One of her employees was a chronic complainer, who always had something negative to say. He had already sent a letter to Nancy's boss complaining about her treatment of her employees. Another employee was very sensitive and felt Nancy was overly harsh.

A coaching consultant was called in by Nancy because the atmosphere in the branch office had become very tense and overall performance had deteriorated.

The good news was that Nancy was receptive to learning a new way to manage. The consultant and she decided together that Nancy needed to learn more options for dealing with her employees and that the work group as a whole needed to learn how to work together as a collaborative team.

The consultant coached Nancy on what it meant to be a coach and showed her ways to facilitate team meetings so that the onus of accountability and success became a group responsibility.

Within a short time, the atmosphere of Nancy's branch started to change for the better. The interpersonal tension was gone. Nancy took a new tack in the way she related to her employees. She began to let go of her compulsion to control every aspect of the workflow by delegating more and letting her employees find their own best way to do the job, not just her way. She met more regularly with individual employees and began guiding them in a non-confrontational way. She spread responsibility around the team. She created a new position of sales team leader and elevated her top performer to that position. She didn't relax her sales goals, but she included the team in the process of developing these goals.

The team meetings stopped being administrative meetings where Nancy just passed on information. They became opportunities for an exchange of ideas where issues could be dealt with honestly and fully. New ideas were explored and responsibilities delegated. Nancy met more frequently with each employee to see how she could help them build their individual strengths and work better within the overall team. After four months, the performance of the office was on the upswing.

◆ ◆ ◆ ◆ ◆ ◆ ◆

Anyone can learn how to be an effective coach. Coaching involves helping a person perform more effectively through a positive interaction that evokes growth and behavioral change. Stated simply, coaching involves interactions that promote learning to improve performance.

Coaching involves . . .

interactions that promote learning to improve performance.

How will learning about coaching help you as a manager? Regardless of how experienced a manager is, he or she risks becoming stuck in the same old pattern of responding, particularly when the employees are experienced, long-term, effective workers. It can almost seem that you are following a script together. The risk is getting too comfortable and familiar.

The job of the manager as coach is to help others avoid becoming stuck or too comfortable in the routine aspects of their work. The manager as coach can help employees discover how to embrace growth and learning on the job.

To become a good coach to motivate and develop your employees, you first have to look at yourself.

You can start by honestly answering the questions on the following page. Write out your responses to assess how you can grow as a manager.

Self-Assessment Questions

1. What are my strengths and weaknesses as a manager?

   _____

   _____

   _____

   _____

2. How can I better optimize my strengths and challenge my weaknesses?

   _____

   _____

   _____

   _____

3. In what ways have I become too complacent?

   _____

   _____

   _____

   _____

4. How do I stereotype my employees?

   _____

   _____

   _____

   _____

Taking on the role of a coach can help you improve in the areas covered by the self-assessment. Your answers will give you an idea of where you specifically need to develop as a manager.

Recognizing how you need to grow and develop as a manager opens the door to learning how to take on the role of coach in your work. Let's find out how the role of coach can be incorporated into the other roles of a manager.

Different Roles for Managers

A manager wears several different hats. Managing involves many different roles. Some of these include:

1. *Planner*—determining strategies and use of resources.

2. *Problem Solver*—making decisions and resolving difficulties.

3. *Information Handler*—disseminating relevant information: both that which is specific to the immediate work group and that which relates to the organization as a whole.

4. *Director*—assigning specific duties and tasks to subordinates.

5. *Coach*—developing the technical, personal, and interpersonal skills of employees.

In reality, these roles constantly blend into one another, and the role of coach overlaps each of the manager's other roles, as shown by the following diagram.

Different Roles for Managers

In order to enhance employee development, it's important to keep the role of coach at the forefront of your mind. Then, even when taking on another role, you are always looking for opportunities to coach.

Let's look at some opportunities for taking on the coaching role while you are in one of the other four management roles.

The Planner Role

One management role is that of planner.

Planner Behaviors

❖ Visioning
❖ Strategizing
❖ Setting Goals

Planning is important because it creates a cohesive structure for the work of the group. Effective managers find the time to plan on a regular basis. They plan by following these three steps:

1. Developing a vision, a picture of what they want to accomplish.

2. Creating specific long-term strategies for achieving the vision.

3. Concretizing the strategies by developing clear short-term goals.

Planner and Coach

When in the planning role, you can still take a coaching perspective by including in your vision a picture of what your employees can become in the future. Thus, your strategies and short-term goals will include the developmental needs of your employees.

➥ Case Example

Beth Bennett, Division Director of the Guest Rooms Division
at a luxury hotel, was developing a one-year plan for her division.
She envisioned a level of customer service that left an indelible
impression of excellence with the hotel guests. Imbedded within
that vision was a new level of effectiveness for all the employees
in her division. She thought specifically of the managers under
her direct supervision and how they could reach new heights in
their skills and abilities. This coaching viewpoint was carried
through into her strategies and goals for the year.

One strategy was to expand the areas of responsibility for each of
her subordinates. Specific goals included what new areas would
be taken on and when.

♦ ♦ ♦ ♦ ♦ ♦ ♦

The Problem Solver Role

Another management role is that of problem solver.

Problem Solver Behaviors

❖ Identifying
❖ Exploring
❖ Resolving

A manager's day consists of a continual stream of problems and challenges. Some are unexpected and others are recurrent issues. Sometimes the trick is to avoid solving every problem too quickly.

Problem solving follows these three steps:

1. Clearly identifying the issue.

2. Thoroughly exploring the full range of alternatives for solving a problem.

3. Resolving the challenge in an orderly and well-considered manner.

Problem Solver and Coach

A limited view of being a problem solver is to think that the only goal is to resolve the immediate problem. When you take the perspective of problem solver and coach, you think about solving a problem in such a way that your employees participate in devising the solution and, thus, have new opportunities to grow.

The solution may not be identical to the one you would have decided upon had you acted independently. However, the benefit to the organization will be much greater because you have not only solved the problem but you have contributed to the long-term strength of your team.

➥ Case Example

Octavio Burk, Operations Manager at a mid-size defense contracting company, was working on the relocation of a branch of 50 employees onto a new floor of the company's office building. It was a touchy situation because there were a limited number of offices with windows and some people would have to move from small offices to cubicles.

Octavio was also feeling pressured because he was involved in a major planning project with the other senior managers.

One of Octavio's direct reports was Carl Lawrence. He thought that this situation would be a good opportunity for Carl to grow in his interpersonal skills by becoming more assertive and direct with others.

Octavio had certain ideas about how to solve the relocation problem, but he asked Carl how he would handle it. Carl's approach to the problem was not exactly the same as Octavio's approach, but Octavio saw it would get the job done in a satisfactory manner. He gave Carl the assignment with the understanding he would check in with him before he began each major step of the project. By carefully guiding Carl in how to communicate with other employees as he encountered different difficulties, Octavio was able to take advantage of a good learning opportunity and the problem was solved.

♦ ♦ ♦ ♦ ♦ ♦ ♦

The Information Handler Role

A third management role is that of information handler.

Information Handler Behaviors

❖ Monitoring
❖ Informing
❖ Recording

Information is the lifeblood of every organization. As an information handler, the manager needs to practice:

1. *Monitoring*—systematically keeping an eye on the information emanating from within and outside his or her workgroup.

2. *Informing*—sharing information orally or in written form.

3. *Recording*—methodically writing down relevant information.

Information Handler and Coach

Doing a good job at handling information means knowing who needs to know what and when. Taking a coaching perspective when sharing information may mean sharing more information than you otherwise might because you want to help your subordinates understand and learn from a situation.

➥ Case Example

Pearl Clover was a Manager at a software development company. Her section was responsible for creating a web interface for one of the company's most popular products. One of her employees, Ben Farly, was deciding how to develop a particular service based on the limited information at Ben's disposal. Ben wasn't aware of a potential upcoming budget shortfall as well as the preference of upper management toward a particular course of action.

Pearl shared the information with Ben and coached him into a new decision based on the broader perspective of the budgetary and political information.

♦ ♦ ♦ ♦ ♦ ♦ ♦

21

The Director Role

Another role for managers is that of director.

Director Behaviors

❖ Telling
❖ Dictating
❖ Controlling

Directing involves:

1. *Telling*—ordering people by giving specific instructions about what to do.

2. *Dictating*—commanding a particular action.

3. *Controlling*—determining the direction.

Directing is good for setting the overall framework for whatever an employee needs to do. Directing every step of a course of action is important when there is a time-sensitive situation or an emergency where quick action is called for.

Director and Coach

When you are dealing with an urgent situation that requires a snap decision, you can still tailor instructions to subordinates in ways that help them grow.

➡ Case Example

Arjuna Singh was the Manager of Creative Services at an advertising agency. His team was given a 48-hour deadline to come up with a presentation to try to land a huge job with a Fortune 500 company. Arjuna needed to decide who was going to handle what part of the project.

Arjuna immediately assigned to Carol Jones, his top creative specialist, the job of coming up with the main ideas. He was going to ask his next best person, Steve Garson, to assist, but decided his new employee, Bob Johnson, was ready to take on more responsibility, and so he gave Bob the key assistant role. Arjuna had also been aware that Steve was in need of more management experience, so Arjuna had Steve take over running an important project Carol had been in charge of that involved overseeing three other employees.

◆ ◆ ◆ ◆ ◆ ◆ ◆

Let's review **the different roles for managers**.

A manager has many different roles. These include:

Planner Role
❖ Visioning
❖ Strategizing
❖ Setting Goals

Problem Solver Role
❖ Identifying
❖ Exploring
❖ Resolving

Information Handler Role
❖ Monitoring
❖ Informing
❖ Recording

Director Role
❖ Telling
❖ Dictating
❖ Controlling

In reality, these roles are constantly blending into each other. To become a workplace coach, you should keep the role of *coach* at the forefront of your mind so that even when taking on another role, you are looking for opportunities to coach your employees.

Coaching Pitfalls

There are various pitfalls that keep managers from being effective coaches.

False Praise

When you give praise that you don't really believe, your subordinate will know it.

Perfectionism

If you are too picky and directive about performance, the employee will stop trying.

Vague Feedback

Generalizations and unclear feedback will have limited impact.

Inconsistency

Sending mixed messages about goals and expectations can lead to confusion and/or resentment.

Constant Criticism

This is not coaching! It is punishment and punishment stops an employee from taking any creative, independent action.

Being Uninvolved

You can't help someone develop without participation and interest in his or her work.

Ignoring a Problem

Letting a problem fester will only make it worse and will not contribute to employee growth.

The way to overcome these pitfalls is to begin to operate at work with the approach of a coach.

SECTION 2
THE APPROACH OF A COACH

Effective coaching entails having a particular approach or point of view.

A good coach:

1. Is deliberate and prepared.

2. Makes the coaching process mutual.

3. Strives to be a great communicator.

4. Is always looking for opportunities to coach.

5. Builds a coaching environment.

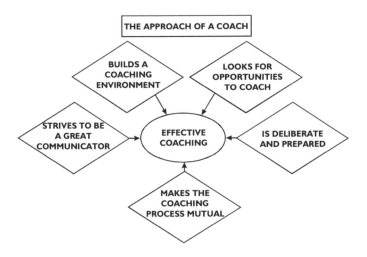

A Coach Is Deliberate and Prepared

It takes a deliberate effort to be an effective coach. And this deliberate effort has its optimal effect when you take the time to prepare.

To be deliberate and prepared:

1. Understand the reasons for coaching and have clear goals for the employee's development.

2. Take the time to plan how to approach the employee.

3. Keep a written record.

Understand the Reasons for Coaching and Have Clear Goals

Analyze the information you've gathered to get a clear picture of the person and his or her performance needs.

Define the developmental goals you want to accomplish when coaching the employee (more on goals on page 63).

Take the Time to Plan How to Approach the Employee

Think about your overall game plan for how you want to coach the employee. Do you want to start with a formal coaching meeting, agreeing on the ground rules? Do you want to be more casual and start in an informal setting?

Keep a Written Record

Keep a record of your perceptions and performance plans for your employee. It doesn't have to be extensive, but it can serve as a valuable resource for staying on target in helping the employee and could be useful if there's a need to document interactions in the future. It keeps you, as a coach, on your game plan for developing the employee, and it gives you a clear record for any corrective actions at a later date.

➡ Case Example

Frank Able, Media Manager for a public relations firm, sat down to think about how to coach his new Communications Specialist, Judy Smith. It had been a long day and he was tired, but Judy had been there three weeks and Frank wanted to prepare his plan of action for how to coach Judy. He wrote up a summary of what he knew about Judy thus far and identified some specific developmental goals for her. Frank thought Judy had great potential, but she seemed to have some difficulty when dealing with clients.

A co-worker had mentioned to Frank that Judy seemed tense and strained in a client meeting. So Frank sat in on several of Judy's meetings involving clients. He did observe that Judy was overly tense and nervous in dealing with clients.

His first step was getting Judy to acknowledge the problem. He decided to ask her perspective about how the meetings went. He planned to then mention specific comments she made to the client and ask what she was thinking at the time and how she thought she was perceived by the client. This would lead into ways she could improve her client contact skills.

♦ ♦ ♦ ♦ ♦ ♦ ♦

A Coach Strives to Be a Great Communicator

Coaching involves communicating in spoken or written form. Thus, effective communication skills are critical.

Communication is never an exact experience because the message goes through a series of filters. Let's review the communication process.

The Communication Process

The process goes like this:

❖ I've got something I want to communicate, so I'm acting as the message sender. This message goes through my filters. I form that message into certain words and nonverbal signals that I send outwards. This selection affects the message. So this first set of filters modifies my "pure" message.

❖ Then the message goes to the person with whom I am trying to communicate. What has been sent goes through the receiver's filters. These filters interpret what they perceive, attending to certain aspects of the message and modifying this interpretation based upon past experience and cognitive constructs. So there is never any pure, direct communication.

Because communication is never direct—going through these two sets of filters—it is never completely exact. A good coach is aware of this process and works to reduce the distortions that occur because of the filters.

At work, communication distortions occur for a wide variety of reasons. Let's explore what factors contribute to your communication distortions.

Factors Leading to Communication Distortions

List the factors that cause communication distortions for you.

Examples:

❖ I'm too busy to focus on what someone is saying.

❖ I prejudge how someone will respond to what I say.

1. _____

   _____

2. _____

   _____

3. _____

   _____

4. _____

   _____

5. _____

   _____

Let's explore how to go beyond these distortions.

To be a good communicator you need to be able to:

1. Read and empathize with others.
2. Communicate with flexibility.

Reading Others

Reading others means the ability to be aware of, understand, and appreciate the feelings of others.

Studies have found that when you show that you understand and appreciate others, they will reciprocate the feeling. Reading others creates a connectedness between people that leads to greater communication and effectiveness.

When we read others, we are able to tune in to the other person. Being able to read others means we can understand them better and respond to their needs or goals. Reading others builds trust. That is why it is crucial for an effective coaching relationship.

To fully receive the message others are sending, we need to:

1. Let go of our personal agenda.
2. Stay focused.
3. Pay attention to nonverbal messages.

Much of our emotional communication is nonverbal. In other words, when we get an emotional message from another person, much of that message comes in some form other than the actual words spoken. It could be in the way it is spoken, called the paralinguistic cues, like the tone or volume of the voice. It could be in body language, facial gestures, posture, or hand gestures. If we allow ourselves to be aware of it, there is much information to be gleaned from nonverbal communication.

When we are open to others' feelings and when we invite a reaction, we can better tune in to others and have positive influence over them.

Research has shown that there are a variety of mechanisms that take place in humans for the development of their ability to read others. They include:

❖ Remembering your own similar experience.

❖ Putting yourself in the other person's place by imagining that what is happening to that person is happening to you.

❖ Contemplating how the other person must feel in the situation.

Communicating with Flexibility

Communicating with flexibility is having a full range of emotional expression and being able to adapt what you say based on what's best for the situation. It's knowing when to express your genuine emotions and when to modify or suppress their expression depending on the circumstances. It's about communicating in a way that shows respect for others as well as for yourself. Making the effort to express yourself flexibly helps you optimize the coaching experience.

Two ingredients for communicating with flexibility follow:

Showing emotion

It can be constructive to show your emotion. It's a way to share information. This does not mean that you have to do it aggressively. When you show how you feel about a situation, you bring heightened awareness to areas an employee needs to develop in an assertive and helpful way.

Being appropriately honest

Timing is important when you are giving feedback. Being too blunt can cause an employee to shut down. Another way to approach it is to practice *planned* honesty.

➥ Case Example

Let's revisit Frank Able and Judy Smith at the public relations firm. Frank was getting to know Judy better. He had the sense that Judy had strong opinions, took pride in her work, and at times might be overly perfectionistic. Frank made a point to be very respectful of Judy's ideas and gave Judy plenty of room to make decisions relevant to her sphere of responsibility. However, at times Frank felt that Judy responded to co-workers in a caustic manner.

Within earshot of Frank, Judy told Bob, a co-worker, that his suggestion for solving a problem was "a stupid idea."

Frank waited until he could speak with Judy alone, and then he said, "You seemed to have a strong reaction to Bob's idea. Tell me what bothers you."

Judy replied, "It would never have worked and was a waste of time."

Frank said, "If that had been me, I would have been really put off by the way you said it, not that you disagreed with my idea. It concerns me that you respond stronger than necessary at times. Why do you think you do that?"

Judy said, "Bob really gets on my nerves because he always has to have his say."

Frank answered, "I've observed you react that way with other people. I think this would be good for us to explore further as an area for you to grow in. Are you willing to look at this further to help you be more effective with others?"

Judy said, "OK, but I don't think it's such a big deal."

Frank said, "What say this week we pay attention to *when* you do it and the reactions you get from others. Then we could touch base about it during our weekly meeting next week."

♦ ♦ ♦ ♦ ♦ ♦ ♦

A Coach Makes the Coaching Process Mutual

Coaching needs to be a mutual process to be most effective. It's not about dictating to someone; it's working together for growth. Key to making the coaching relationship mutual is respect. The power of respect is not only in being polite (although this makes for smoother conversations), but in truly seeing the other person as important and multi-faceted. If you are limited in how you view your employees and do not respect them for who they are, then your impact as a coach will be limited.

To make the coaching process mutual:

1. Have a balanced give and take.

2. See mistakes as learning opportunities.

3. Be available and accessible.

4. Make agreements.

5. Follow through on your commitments.

Have a Balanced Give and Take

Don't do all the talking. Make room for the employee's thoughts and reactions. Discover his or her perspective, what motivates that person, and what his or her goals are.

See Mistakes as Learning Opportunities

Everybody makes mistakes. The trick is to benefit from them. Don't attack a person who makes a mistake or put him or her down. Instead, have a discussion immediately after the mistake happens to determine the employee's experiences and reactions. Study the actions that were taken and explore what else might have been done.

Be Available and Accessible

Coaching is an ongoing process. Let your employee know clearly how and when he or she can speak with you.

Make Agreements

Whenever you have a formal or informal coaching interaction, make sure you end it with a clear agreement: "So you are going to increase your cold calling by contacting at least 10 new leads everyday. You'll keep track in your contact log and tell me about any of the leads that seem to have potential."

Follow up on topics discussed. Let your employee know that you want to be kept informed about how it is going.

Follow Through on Your Commitments

When you make commitments to your employees, make sure that you honor them. In this way, they will be more likely to follow through on their commitment. Part of coaching is modeling the qualities that you wish to develop in your employees.

➡ Case Example

Arthur Hanson had made his first big mistake at his new job as a production manager for a lighting supplies company. He had implemented a marketing plan for a product before production was great enough to support new demand. Customers were upset because delivery was very delayed.

His boss, Evelyn Trey, called a meeting to discuss the issue. Evelyn started the conversation by asking Arthur what happened. Evelyn didn't say much at the beginning of the meeting; she listened calmly to what Arthur had to say, occasionally asking questions about the decision-making process.

They came to the conclusion that Arthur needed to get a clearer understanding about the production process and how it interfaced with the role-out of a marketing plan. They agreed that over the next few weeks Arthur would spend time observing the production process and increase his communication with the production staff. Arthur and Evelyn would meet weekly to discuss what Arthur had learned, and Evelyn would share with Arthur examples of successful marketing plans Evelyn had initiated in the past.

Evelyn told Arthur that if he had any questions about his next marketing plan, he shouldn't hesitate to contact or visit her.

♦ ♦ ♦ ♦ ♦ ♦ ♦

A Coach Is Always Looking for Opportunities to Coach

Three variables are important in seeking opportunities to coach. They are:

1. The focus.

2. The setting.

3. The timing.

The Focus

There are numerous occasions when coaching can be initiated.

Any type of change within the work environment

Coaching can occur whenever a shift in the status quo occurs. This might include new hires, new standards, or a change in work responsibilities.

To reinforce positive performance

Coaching helps employees to identify which actions they should continue and build upon.

To deal with performance problems

This includes when a person doesn't know how to do the job. For example, an employee fails to organize his workload effectively.

Performance problems also occur when a person doesn't want to do the job. For example, an employee seems to hide behind his office door and only produces a fraction of his colleague's output.

The Setting

Coaching can occur in a formal or informal setting. The two can be connected. Topics discussed in a formal meeting can be referred to during informal meetings. For example, if in a formal setting you had previously discussed ways the employee could more actively explore a customer's needs, listen in on a customer call made by the employee and discuss it together afterwards.

A formal setting

A formal setting is where there is a scheduled meeting in an office, conference room, or over the phone, with a structured format. For example, conducting a performance appraisal.

An informal setting

An informal setting can be anywhere: walking in the hallway, driving in the car, standing by the employee's desk.

The Timing

Although almost any situation may offer an opportunity to coach, it is important to recognize if the time is right.

Check your mindset

You need to make sure you are in the right frame of mind to coach. If you are impatient for action or unsure of what needs to happen, coaching attempts could create negative consequences.

Identify the employee's readiness

Determine if the employee is receptive to coaching at that moment. If he or she is feeling particularly insecure, off balance, or too focused on a task to listen, coaching may be detrimental at that moment.

See if the situation is ripe

Sometimes you need to give the employee time to get further into a challenge before you start to coach. The more data you have about how the person handles a task, the clearer your feedback can be.

➡ Case Example

Lanny Green, the Senior E-Commerce Manager in the Information Technology Department of a network systems facility, was upset. Lanny just found out that one of his employees, Hank Parkman, had caused a glitch in the network of a major customer. He was irritated and disappointed. He rushed over to assess the situation and found Hank focused on making the corrections to get the system up and going. The network would be back up soon. Instead of going ahead at that moment and discussing the mistake, Lanny decided to wait until after Hank was finished with the project. He recognized that the time was not right because he was upset and Hank needed to focus on what he was doing.

Later, when he was calmer and Hank was free, Lanny called him into his office to have a quiet discussion about how the mistake happened and how Hank could learn from the experience.

♦ ♦ ♦ ♦ ♦ ♦ ♦

A Coach Builds a Coaching Environment

Creating a climate that supports coaching maximizes your effectiveness as a coach.

Three elements of an effective coaching environment are:

1. Positive reinforcement and motivation.

2. Giving change time.

3. Encouraging growth.

Positive Reinforcement and Motivation

Positive reinforcement does not only occur with a big bonus check at the end of the year. A good coach finds small ways to reinforce and motivate employees frequently and regularly.

There are many modes to reinforce and motivate someone beyond monetary compensation (although that is always appreciated).

A study by Watson Wyatt, a human resources consulting company, found that 76 percent of employees considered importance of work very significant for motivation. A good coach can help each employee see the importance of his or her work.

Wherever possible, involve subordinates in decision making as it relates to their work areas. Employees want to participate in decisions that involve them and their work.

Praise can range from a brief "It's good" to a very specific "You did a good job on the sales report. It was well thought out and the graphs made it easy to understand."

People also appreciate others hearing about what they have done well. In the same study by Watson Wyatt, a majority of top performers said maintaining a good personal reputation motivates them to achieve peak performance.

You can use a variety of modes to reinforce your employees: voice mail, e-mail, a memo, or a letter of appreciation. The important thing is to let people know they are appreciated.

Giving Change Time

To create an environment for growth, it helps to be realistic about the time frame for change. Impatience and unrealistic expectations create fear and distrust.

Ask yourself this: "How long has it taken me to develop my best skills?" Many skills take months and years to perfect.

Encouraging Growth

Sometimes, when acting in a helping role, we encourage people to do things the way we would do them. However, a person reaches his or her full potential by growing in a manner consistent with his or her own perspectives, talents, and inclinations. Take the time to discover and nurture the uniqueness in each employee.

➠ Case Example

Ann Zachery, Engineering Manager at a glass manufacturing company, had now been supervising Ellen Bassett for eight months. She reviewed how Ellen had progressed. She noted that Ellen had improved her communication skills with her colleagues. Ellen still had a tendency to spend too much time on the details of her work and not enough time looking at the bigger picture.

They had developed a good working relationship. Ann regularly gave Ellen positive reinforcement casually throughout the day and in their once-a-week meetings. Ann figured it was time to look for new ways for Ellen to grow in her job. Ann invited Ellen to offer her ideas about new directions in which she would like to grow. Together, they sketched out what new skills and responsibilities Ellen could develop over the next six months.

◆ ◆ ◆ ◆ ◆ ◆ ◆

Let's review **the approach of a coach.**

A Coach Is Deliberate and Prepared
❖ Understands the reasons for coaching and has clear goals
❖ Takes the time to plan how to approach the employee
❖ Keeps a written record

A Coach Strives to Be a Great Communicator
❖ Reads others
  • By being alert to the signs of emotions in others
❖ Communicates with flexibility
  • By showing emotion
  • By being appropriately honest

A Coach Makes the Coaching Process Mutual
❖ Has a balanced give and take
❖ Sees mistakes as learning opportunities
❖ Is available and accessible
❖ Makes agreements
❖ Follows through on his or her commitments

A Coach Is Always Looking for Opportunities to Coach
❖ The focus
  • Any type of change
  • To reinforce positive performance
  • To deal with performance problems
❖ The setting
  • Formal setting
  • Informal setting
❖ The timing
  • Checks his or her mindset
  • Identifies the employee's readiness
  • Determines when the situation is ripe

A Coach Builds a Coaching Environment
- ❖ Positively reinforces and motivates
- ❖ Gives change time
- ❖ Encourages growth

Applying the Approach of a Coach

Now we'll practice how to take the approach of a coach by looking at possible responses to the following situation. After reviewing the different responses to the scenario, identify which aspects of the approach of a coach are or are not exemplified in the answers.

A new employee has just joined your staff. He has made a big error in a key report that was reviewed by senior management. You say:

A. "Don't ever do that again. We'll talk about this more during your 30-day review."

B. "When we're both free this afternoon, let's meet to debrief how the mistake happened and how we can help you to do better the next time."

C. "You've got me so angry. Just don't talk to me for the next week."

D. "You seem upset about what happened. Tell me exactly what happened."

E. "I'm concerned about this mistake. I hope to be able to smooth it over with top management. Why don't we meet tomorrow after we've both cooled down to figure out how we can avoid this type of problem in the future."

Evaluating the Responses

Response A:

"Don't ever do that again. We'll talk about this more during your 30-day review."

This response is a dictatorial, attacking, "I'm the boss" style. In no way is it coaching because it is not deliberate, prepared, mutual, attentive to the other person, or positive.

Response B:

"When we're both free this afternoon, let's meet to debrief how the mistake happened and how we can help you to do better the next time."

In addressing the performance problem, this manager is setting up a formal meeting at an appropriate time. The response also shows that the manager views the mistake as a learning opportunity.

Response C:

"You've got me so angry. Just don't talk to me for the next week."

This is an off-the-cuff response from the manager that shows inappropriate expression of emotion. There is no attempt to gather information about what happened.

Response D:

"You seem upset about what happened. Tell me exactly what happened."

This response shows foresight by the manager and an ability to read the reaction of the employee. There is an implied readiness to give the employee time to deal with the situation.

Response E:

"I'm concerned about this mistake. I hope to be able to smooth it over with top management. Why don't we meet tomorrow after we've both cooled down to figure out how we can avoid this type of problem in the future."

This response shows appropriate expression of emotion and acknowledges the need to take time to figure out the problem. It indicates a mutual involvement in the problem.

SECTION 3
THE COACHING PROCESS

There are several elements to the coaching process. These elements don't necessarily unfold in a linear, clearly defined manner. It is useful to understand each element and to learn how to develop the abilities relevant to each.

1. Gathering information

2. Setting the stage

3. Encouraging self-assessment

4. Clarifying goals

5. Exploring perspective

6. Creating a feedback loop

7. Knowing when to move on

Gathering Information

Make sure you have all the facts about how the employee is handling different situations and interacting with others. You can get this information by keeping a "sharp eye" out during the workday and studying performance data.

On-Site Observation

To gain better insight into the strengths and weaknesses of employees, join them during part of their day. Go with them when they deal with clients or sit with them at their desk. Be very clear about the purpose of your presence and be supportive and observant rather than jumping into what the person is doing.

Find Out How the Employee Thinks

Purposefully explore the "why" behind the person's actions. Use pinpointing questions (see page 80) to go deeper into the person's perspective and motivation.

Coaching Tips

Delay evaluation

Keep an open mind

Check out assumptions

Setting the Stage

The First Time

When you first start to work with an employee, spell out the process of coaching. Explain its importance and relevance to success. Clearly state how you like to operate as a coach. Find out how the employee feels about the coaching process and how he or she likes to work.

In a Formal Coaching Meeting

When you are having a formal coaching meeting, establish the structure for the session. Say something like, "I would like to meet today for half an hour to review and discuss how your work is going."

In an Informal Coaching Meeting

In an informal situation, you could say something like, "Let's take a minute to talk about the DSI job. I want to get your take and debrief what happened. What's your perspective on the project?"

Frame the Time for Talking

It can be very useful to create a set of communication agreements consciously and deliberately that support active listening.

Underlying all the agreements is the goal of promoting an atmosphere of mutual respect.

If you are the initiator, always start with a question like, "Can you talk?" or "Is this a good time for a question?"

Coaching Tips

Be flexible

Don't jump to solutions

Make sure you and the employee are in agreement

Encouraging Self-Assessment

Ask the employee how he or she rates him- or herself on different skills and abilities.

Regular Self-Observation

Give the employee a week to observe him- or herself. Then have the employee report back specific examples of when he or she was effective and when difficulties arose. An employee can keep a daily log or a checklist of specific performance areas to observe.

Focus on All Aspects of Performance

Look beyond the end result. Invite the employee to look at how he or she made the intermediate decisions leading up to the final action.

Self-awareness is a key skill for employees to become life-long learners. Building self-awareness makes coaching much easier by opening the door to self-directed growth.

Coaching Tips

Be non-judgmental

Go deeper into the "whys" behind the employee's actions

Share examples from your experience

Clarifying Goals

Delineate what areas you specifically want to address through coaching. Identify specific performance goals you want to reach. This should be an ongoing process.

Identify Technical and Process Developmental Goals

In general, performance can be broken down into the broad categories of *technical* skills and *process* skills. Technical skills pertain to the specific work tasks associated with a particular job, such as word processing or budget analysis. Process skills refer to the way work gets done. These would include interpersonal dealings with colleagues and customers, flexibility, managing reactions, determination, etc.

Coaching Tips

Create short-term steps to reach long-term goals

Focus on performance and results

Exploring Perspective

Watch Out for Limiting Assumptions

It is very easy to get stuck in the assumption that our beliefs are the ultimate truth. A coach can be instrumental in helping an employee recognize limiting assumptions. By gently challenging his or her perspective in a given situation, you help the other person grow.

Discovering New Outlooks

The broader the perspective we can take about a situation, the more likely it is that we will be effective. The coach can share his or her perspective of a situation and invite the employee to solicit others' perspectives. The more feedback there is about the different ways to view a situation, the more options there are for a new outlook.

Coaching Tips

Guide rather than dictate

Wait for the employee to understand your point

Suggest relevant reading material to encourage new perspectives

---

Creating a Feedback Loop

A feedback loop is a system for the continuous return of information concerning the result of a process. It's very important to be able to evaluate changes in the areas selected for development. Review your coaching goals to help you determine the best performance measures. Specific measures would include short-term deliverables and underlying processes in the employee's workflow.

Discuss with the employee the best ways to measure improvement and growth. Make it part of your coaching conversation.

Coaching Tips

Use multiple sources of information

Look for improvement, not perfection

Knowing When to Move On

An important part of the coaching process is knowing when to stop focusing on a developmental area and move on to something else. Ultimately, as the employee reaches a high level of competence, coaching can slow down or mostly phase out. The coaching relationship will change as the employee changes and as the coach changes. The coach needs to be aware of these changes and take responsibility for adjusting the relationship accordingly.

Coaching Tips

Recognize mastery of a skill

Look for new goals

Know when to let go

➡ Case Example

Cassandra Scott, Team Leader of a web page development team, heard from one of her other staffers that Bob Jenkins, her new graphic artist, had been taking a superior attitude toward some of his teammates and was not producing. Cassandra spoke informally with everyone on her team and asked how Bob was working out. She also reviewed the graphics Bob had produced since coming on board. Cassandra agreed that Bob's performance and attitude needed improvement.

Cassandra scheduled a meeting with Bob, at which she explained her goals as a manager, how she expected the team to perform, and what she expected from Bob. She asked Bob about his style of working, what he enjoyed most about the job, and in which ways Bob wanted to develop professionally. Cassandra proposed that over the next few months they meet once a week to discuss how Bob thought his projects were progressing.

At their next meeting, Cassandra suggested that Bob start keeping a log of his day so that they could discuss it each week. They agreed that each daily entry would focus on two things: (1) How Bob felt he interacted with other team members and what might improve that interaction and (2) How much graphic work he completed that day and what changes would make his day more productive.

As they reviewed Bob's log at their next meeting, Cassandra asked Bob if he saw any change over last week. They discussed what would be considered standards of improvement and agreed that they would review future log entries based on these standards.

During one of their coaching meetings, Cassandra and Bob discussed one of his log entries. Bob felt that when one of the programmers on the team asked him to simplify a particular graphic, it would undermine the quality of the project. Cassandra asked Bob to view the discussion from the programmer's point of view, keeping in mind that complex graphics can hamper a web page's overall performance. After some discussion, Bob agreed that the programmer was not attacking his artistic vision, but was simply speaking from a programming perspective.

After three months, Bob's interaction with his teammates had improved markedly. Based on their weekly reviews, Cassandra provided Bob with some additional tools to increase his performance. Bob's performance was now nearly equal to that of the veteran graphic artists on the team. Cassandra decided that there was no longer a need for the weekly coaching sessions and let Bob know that though her door was always open, they could start meeting on an as-needed basis.

♦ ♦ ♦ ♦ ♦ ♦ ♦

Let's review **the elements of the coaching process**.

The elements of the coaching process are:

❖ **Gathering information**

❖ **Setting the stage**

❖ **Encouraging self-assessment**

❖ **Clarifying goals**

❖ **Exploring perspective**

❖ **Creating a feedback loop**

❖ **Knowing when to move on**

SECTION 4
COACHING CONVERSATION SKILLS

The coaching conversation is at the heart of successful coaching. Here are a set of important skills to acquire for having an effective coaching conversation.

1. Focused listening

2. Paraphrasing

3. Reflection of feeling

4. Active inquiry

5. Giving feedback

6. Process communication

7. Summarizing

8. Using silence

Focused Listening

One of the most important components of effective coaching is listening. In a study by Loyola University, employees from hundreds of businesses across the country were asked, "What is the most important attribute of an effective manager?" The most highly rated skill was listening.

Everyone recognizes the importance of good listening, but many people do not always act on this recognition. Some of the mind-sets that stop us from effective listening are:

❖ I have too much to do.

❖ I'm tired.

❖ It takes too long.

❖ It's hard work.

❖ There are too many distractions.

❖ I want to do the talking.

When under pressure, we have a tendency to stop listening. It becomes a vicious circle. We feel more pressure at work and don't have as much time to listen. Not listening leads to greater problems in achieving results, so it creates greater pressure.

Focused listening means paying concentrated attention to what someone else is saying. We first need to pay attention to what is going on with the other person. To do this we must let go of our personal agenda and choose to focus on them.

It is important to recognize that *listening is different from agreeing*. Another point to recognize is that *we speak more slowly than we think,* so we can use this extra thinking time to go deeper into the other person's message.

Here are the steps to focused listening.

Expand Your Reception

Be open to picking up all possible information. Be aware of the subtle shades of meaning being expressed. When you have the impulse to interrupt or insert your opinion, ask a question instead to further understand the other's point of view.

Step into the Other Person's Shoes

Imagine yourself in the other person's place. Think about how he or she must feel about what he or she is describing.

Dig Deeper into the Message

Use your extra thinking time to hypothesize about what is the core message of what's being communicated.

Paraphrasing

Paraphrasing is repeating what you heard, in your own words.

It's not just parroting back to the person. It's repeating what you heard in a way that shows you really understand.

For example:

"What I heard you say was that when Accounting delays approving your budget, you feel stuck. Is that right?"

Reflection of Feeling

Reflection of feeling is expressing your understanding of what you think the speaker is experiencing.

When you acknowledge an employee's feelings, it helps you to connect with and understand the speaker.

For example:

"As you talk about your assistant, you sound very frustrated and angry. Is that correct?"

Active Inquiry

Active inquiry means making the effort to get a deeper understanding of someone through questioning.

Two forms of active inquiry are:

❖ Open-ended questions.

❖ Pinpointing questions.

Open-ended vs. Closed-ended Questions

Open-ended questions are those that generate elaborate responses. They promote more conversation. Closed-ended questions lead to one-word answers like "yes or no," which can be OK if you are just fact finding or clarifying, but not when you're doing active inquiry.

Here are some examples of closed-ended questions:

❖ "Did you finish the assignment?"

❖ "Do you understand the new regulations?"

Here are some examples of open-ended questions:

❖ "How do you think we could do this assignment better?"

❖ "Where could we make improvements in our new organizational plan?"

❖ "What problems do you think we'll run into with this idea?"

Pinpointing Questions

These are questions used to pinpoint meaning, intent, direction, and relevance. They focus the conversation in a way that brings greater clarity to the issue under discussion.

Examples of pinpointing questions are:

❖ "Can you talk about what makes it difficult to say what you are thinking?"

❖ "What specific results are you trying to achieve?"

❖ "Exactly how does this relate to the problem at hand?"

Giving Feedback

When giving feedback, make sure that you are doing it in the most uplifting way possible. Remember that the goal of coaching is to help the employee grow in a way that benefits the organization and all individuals involved. Feedback given from an orientation of superiority, anger, or disapproval will spark defensiveness and limit the benefit of the feedback.

Guidelines for Giving Constructive Feedback to Employees

1. Make sure the feedback is necessary and beneficial.

2. Focus on behavior that can be observed.

3. Turn negative feedback into an opportunity for learning.

4. Negative feedback should include specific suggestions for how the employee can improve.

5. Don't over generalize. Avoid saying "you always" or "you never."

6. Own your feedback. Use "I" statements rather than "you" statements. Stay away from *"the organization* thinks" and "*we* believe."

7. Focus feedback on behavior the person can change.

8. Mix positive with negative feedback.

9. Get feedback about your feedback.

Applying the Guidelines for Giving Constructive Feedback

Let's practice giving feedback by reviewing different responses to the following situation. Identify which feedback guidelines are or are not exemplified in the answers.

You are the Manager of Technical Recruiting for a biotech company. One of your recruiters, Dominic Solimene, is good at gathering information about potential job candidates, but has difficulty selling the company to them. When you previously sat in on Dominic's interviews, you noticed that Dominic was not spending enough time or detail describing the opportunities of the job and the company. You say:

A. "You do a good job in your interviews. Don't forget to sell the company."

B. "Several of the candidates you have interviewed didn't seem convinced about the value they would gain from working for us. What might you do differently to describe the benefits of the company and better enlist good people?"

C. "The organization believes that you're weak in certain areas. We think you need to do a better job in your interviewing. And your accent is distracting."

D. "Dominic, I really appreciate the way you draw information out of the candidates. Like when you asked questions in such a way that it became clear the last fellow was most effective when working with a team of people. I do think you could spend more time focusing on how the company could benefit the candidate. Perhaps you could use your skill at drawing people out to learn what ways our company could best benefit them and use that later on in the interview. Is it clear what I mean?"

Evaluating the Responses

Response A:

"You do a good job in your interviews. Don't forget to sell the company."

This feedback is overly general and does not give any specific suggestions for improvement. Although it mixes positive and negative feedback, Dominic doesn't learn the details of what he did well nor how he could specifically change his behavior to improve his performance.

Response B:

"Several of the candidates you have interviewed didn't seem convinced about the value they would gain from working for us. What might you do differently to describe the benefits of the company and better enlist good people?"

This response gives specific feedback about the problem and opens the door for turning the problem into a learning opportunity.

Response C:

"The organization believes that you're weak in certain areas. We think you need to do a better job in your interviewing. And your accent is distracting."

This response is overly general and the speaker does not own the feedback. Giving feedback about Dominic's accent is bringing up behavior that Dominic cannot change.

Response D:

"Dominic, I really appreciate the way you draw information out of the candidates. Like when you asked questions in such a way that it became clear the last fellow was most effective when working with a team of people. I do think you could spend more time focusing on how the company could benefit the candidate. Perhaps you could use your skill at drawing people out to learn what ways our company could best benefit them and use that later on in the interview. Is it clear what I mean?"

This response focuses on observable behavior and turns the negative feedback into an opportunity for learning. Positive and negative feedback are both included. The feedback includes specific behaviors. The feedback is owned by the speaker and feedback is requested about the feedback.

To help you evaluate your ability to give feedback, take the assessment on the following page. After your next coaching interaction with an employee, rate yourself in the following areas:

Feedback Assessment

Feedback Skill	never	sometimes	often
The feedback was on observable behavior.			
Used "I" statements rather than "you" or "we" statements.			
Focused on specific behavior, not generalizations.			
The feedback was in context.			
Balanced positive and negative feedback.			
Gave specific suggestions for improvement.			
Checked to make sure the message was received.			
Got feedback on the feedback.			

After you have rated yourself, select one or two areas to focus on for self-improvement. When you feel you have reached the level of desired proficiency, then move on to improving another feedback skill.

You can also ask a colleague to fill out the Feedback Assessment sheet to get an outside perspective on your skill level.

Process Communication

The process is the underlying movement behind a conversation. Process is the *way* things are communicated and done. The content is the *topic* of a conversation. Process is usually implicit; content is usually explicit. When we engage in process communication, we shine a light on what's usually important but unspoken. Process comments can be made about an overall situation, underlying patterns, feelings, relationships, or agendas.

Pay Attention to Nonverbal Messages

Nonverbal messages include paralinguistics, body language, facial gestures, posture, and hand gestures.

Identify What Is Happening, Not What Is Being Discussed

This usually involves the manner of communication and the emotions about the interaction.

Make a Clear, Nonattacking Process Comment

Be specific and descriptive.

For example:

"Whenever I bring up the topic of your workload, you seem to tighten up and stop speaking. It makes me think that you are tense and have a problem with your workload. Is this accurate? What do you think it's about?"

Summarizing

Summarizing is making a condensed statement about the substance of what the other person has said over the period of a conversation.

Summarizing rounds out the conversation and assures the other person that you've understood what he or she was talking about.

For example:

"To sum up what we've been discussing, you'd like to take on more responsibility by taking on a bigger scale project. We agreed that I'll keep my eyes open for an appropriate job, and when I find one we'll get together to discuss the possibility of your taking it on. Did that describe what we agreed to?"

Using Silence

It's very useful to know when not to speak. It is one way to keep the focus on the other person to give them the opportunity to expand on their perspective. When the coach is always talking, there is the likelihood that the coach is telling the employee how he or she would do a task, reducing the opportunity for the employee to come up with their own choices.

These eight coaching conversation skills take time and practice to develop. On the following pages is a self-assessment tool for you to identify which skills you need to strengthen.

Conversation Skills Assessment

Use a check mark to rate yourself in the following areas:

Skill Area	poor	average	good
Focused Listening			
Paraphrasing			
Reflection of Feeling			
Active Inquiry			
Giving Feedback			
Process Communication			
Summarizing			
Using Silence			

Note the skill areas in which you gave yourself the lowest scores. Review the techniques relevant to that skill and write a practical action plan for developing the skill.

Action Plan

1. Skill to Develop:

    _____

    Day-to-Day Action Steps:

    _____

    _____

    _____

    Timeline for Development:

    _____

    _____

    _____

2. Skill to Develop:

    _____

    Day-to-Day Action Steps:

    _____

    _____

    _____

    Timeline for Development:

    _____

    _____

    _____

3. Skill to Develop:

_____

Day-to-Day Action Steps:

_____

_____

_____

Timeline for Development:

_____

_____

_____

Let's review.

The coaching conversation skills are:

❖ **Focused listening**

❖ **Paraphrasing**

❖ **Reflection of feeling**

❖ **Active inquiry**

❖ **Giving feedback**

❖ **Process communication**

❖ **Summarizing**

❖ **Using silence**

SECTION 5
TEAM COACHING AND
PEER COACHING

We can maximize overall organizational performance by expanding our definition of coaching beyond the traditional one-on-one supervisory relationship. Coaching can take place within an entire team and between peers.

Team Coaching

A manager can use coaching for the development of an entire team of employees. Team coaching helps create a synergy between employees that contributes to employee satisfaction and excellence in performance.

The two pillars for success in team coaching are:

1. Establishing positive team norms.

2. Running effective meetings.

Establishing and supporting positive team norms serves as the foundation for effective team collaboration. Team meetings are opportunities to bring the norms into play. These norms then carry over beyond group meetings and help foster positive interactions between individual team members.

The interplay of establishing positive team norms, running effective meetings, and how they contribute to the success of the team is demonstrated in the diagram on the following page.

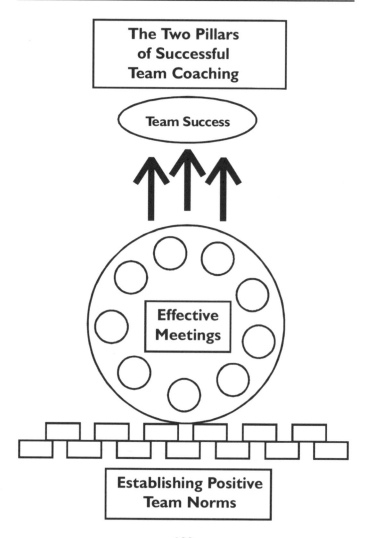

Establishing Positive Team Norms

As a team coach, the focus shifts to the team's accomplishment of its objectives and the development of team capabilities. To do this, you first need to establish the best possible team norms.

Effective team norms include:

1. Shared purpose.

2. Pervasive information sharing.

3. Optimal participation.

4. No hidden agendas.

5. Trust in co-workers.

Shared Purpose

If a group of people has different purposes and goals, they can't operate effectively as a team. A team coach helps communicate the purpose and goals of the team and clarifies the direction for team development.

Pervasive Information Sharing

We've heard that knowledge is power. It takes a concerted effort to ensure optimal communication of information. The team coach should be alert to opportunities for circulating information throughout the team.

Optimal Participation

A high-performing team has everyone collaborating to the best of their abilities. There is a minimum of turf issues and job hoarding. As a team coach, you can encourage ideas, contributions, and suggestions from all team members.

No hidden agendas

Members of an effective team feel free to bring disagreements and conflicts into the open. A team coach invites sharing of honest feedback between employees.

Trust in co-workers

Successful teams operate with an underlying attitude of trust and support. Team members are confident they can rely on others in the team. This attitude starts with the team coach demonstrating trust in the team members.

As a team coach, you can help create these norms by:

1. Regularly talking about the norms you want the team to have.

2. Promoting a safe environment.

3. Encouraging open and honest expression of ideas.

4. Modeling the positive team norms.

5. Including teamwork as an individual performance goal for employees.

Running Effective Meetings

The opportunity to coach the team as a whole takes place in meetings. Running an effective meeting requires clear purpose and structure.

Let's look first at factors that block meeting effectiveness.

Blocks to Meeting Effectiveness

Here are some of the factors that can hinder the effectiveness of a team meeting:

1. Failing to set a clear goal for the meeting.

2. Permitting unbridled interruptions.

3. Too much participation.

4. Too little participation.

5. Not paying attention to what's going on.

6. Ignoring some members of the team.

7. Arguing to win.

8. Personal accusations.

9. Keeping a hidden agenda.

The first step to holding effective meetings is to develop ground rules. Once developed, ground rules serve to keep meetings on track and also help to establish positive team norms that operate beyond meetings.

Ground Rule Development

It is important for a group to agree upon the ground rules for operating as a team. Ground rules lead to an increase in individual accountability.

Following are a number of possible ground rules. Use this list as an example. Let the team suggest its own rules. It is important that there be group consensus about which ground rules will be used for the team.

Possible Meeting Ground Rules

In our team meetings we will:

1. All be responsible for success.
2. Make dealing with disturbances a priority over any other business.
3. Keep contributions short.
4. Make conflicts into a theme.
5. All keep order.
6. Share all relevant information.
7. Test assumptions and inferences.
8. Focus on interests, not positions.
9. Be specific and use examples.
10. Agree on what important words mean.
11. Focus on the situation or issue, not on the person.
12. Explain the reasons behind our statements, questions, and actions.
13. Disagree openly with any member of the group.
14. Keep the discussion focused.
15. Not take cheap shots or otherwise distract the group.
16. All participate in each phase of the process.
17. Make decisions by consensus when possible.
18. Arrive on time and stay for the entire meeting (if late we will put 50 cents in the slush fund).
19. Encourage each other to complete action points.
20. Keep to the meeting agenda.
21. Speak for ourselves (I feel, I think), not others (we feel, we think).

State the Purpose of the Meeting

Whenever a group of employees is called together, it is important to state clearly the *purpose* of the meeting and what you would like the *outcome* of the meeting to be. For example, you might say in an e-mail:

"The purpose of our meeting this Friday from 10 A.M. to 12 noon is to develop a set of ground rules to guide the operation of our team meetings."

When conducting the meeting, the structure can serve as a method for supporting the group norms and ensuring an efficient meeting.

A Structure for Effective Meetings

Define Roles

Have the group select members to perform the following roles:

a. *Timekeeper*—keeps track of time for each phase of the meeting and announces when time is running out.

b. *Minute Taker*—writes out key decisions and action points and distributes them as soon as possible after the meeting.

c. *Scribe*—writes information on the board or flip chart.

d. *Facilitator*—leads the team to accomplish the objectives. Initially the manager can perform this role. As the team begins to take more joint responsibility, this role can be rotated between team members.

Touching Base

This is an opportunity for each team member to briefly share relevant experiences that are happening for him or her personally.

Agree on the Agenda and Prioritize

The agenda will be developed and distributed prior to the meeting. If it is a regular meeting, such as a weekly staff meeting, create the agenda at the end of the previous meeting and have participants add to it during the week. Carry forward any items not dealt with from the previous meeting. Add any current items suggested by members of the group.

Next, list information-sharing topics that should be covered first, since they do not require much discussion. Bunch topics that need to be discussed and processed at the bottom.

Finally, assess how much time the team will spend on each item.

Review Previous Action Points

Go over any action points raised in previous meetings to make sure they are being addressed. This enhances the accountability of the employees.

Sharing and Processing Group Information

This is the heart of the meeting. It's where you address the agenda items. One way to organize this phase of the meeting is to follow the steps to a Structured Round described on page 108.

Plan the Next Meeting and Agenda

Reach a group agreement on when the next meeting will be held and what will be on the agenda. The agenda needs to be made available to all participants in a central location so that they can add agenda items as necessary throughout the week.

Do a Meeting Debrief

Each person provides a one-sentence answer to the questions:

"What did I appreciate about the meeting?"

"What can be improved upon for future meetings?"

To help make sharing and processing group information effective and productive, you can use a structured round. The steps for a structured round are described on the next page.

The Steps for a Structured Round

A structured round is very useful for reaching clarity about a topic and gaining participation from all team members.

1. *Defining a goal.* The topic for the structured round is determined and clearly defined.

2. *Individual work.* Each person silently contemplates and writes down his or her points about the issue under discussion.

3. *Canvassing.* The scribe takes each person's points, one at a time. He or she continues until all items are collected. Points should be kept brief and duplication avoided. Those who don't have any more points may simply say, "Pass."

4. *Clarifying.* The points are reviewed one by one. The person who gave the point can give further information to help the others understand it.

5. *Processing, evaluating, and deciding.* Now that everyone has contributed their ideas, a facilitated discussion takes place to reach the goal. Ideas are grouped under encompassing themes, themes are prioritized, decisions are made, and action plans are developed.

Establishing a clear structure for meetings enhances cooperation and accountability within the team. The team coach works to make sure the ground rules are being followed and everyone participates fully in the team operations.

Peer Coaching

You can teach others to become effective coaches, not only with subordinates, but also with peers. Team members can learn to coach each other.

Employees can demonstrate leadership regardless of the formal position they hold within an organization. Even without any formal authority, they are in a position to inspire and lead others. Peer coaching is an important aspect of leading others.

Successful team coaching helps to create positive team norms. If you have a truly collaborative environment within your organization, there will be a high level of trust and openness. This will set the stage for peer coaching.

Introduce Peer Coaching to the Team

Introduce the idea of peer coaching to the whole team. Stress the importance of asking for feedback from each other.

Meet separately with your top performers and discuss how they can share their knowledge and skills with other employees.

Keep It Informal

Peer coaching tends to be informal and fluid. Of the five elements of *The Approach of a Coach* described earlier in this book, the most important for the peer coach are *striving to be a great communicator* (page 34) and *making the coaching process mutual* (page 40).

Start with a Mutual Agreement

For peer coaching to work, each employee must be fully willing to participate.

Peer coaching might begin with a casual request for feedback from one employee to another.

➥ Case Example

Jorge said, "Jim, I feel stuck with the Big Store program analysis. Could you give me a few minutes to get your take on it?"

Jim answered, "Sure. Send me what you've done so far and then we can get together for a half-hour to talk about it."

When they met, they agreed that Jim will meet with Jorge every few days to review Jorge's progress on that project.

After a few weeks, Jim asked Jorge to coach him on giving a presentation, an area in which Jorge was very proficient.

◆ ◆ ◆ ◆ ◆ ◆ ◆

Let's review **team and peer coaching**.

Team Coaching involves:

❖ **Establishing positive team norms**
  • Shared purpose
  • Pervasive information sharing
  • Optimal participation
  • No hidden agendas
  • Trust in co-workers

❖ **Running effective meetings**
  • Ground rule development
  • State the purpose of the meeting
  • Create an effective meeting structure

Peer Coaching involves:

❖ **Introducing peer coaching to the team**
❖ **Keeping it informal**
❖ **Starting with a mutual agreement**

SECTION 6
DISTANCE COACHING

We have been discussing coaching in situations in which the coach is face-to-face with the employee. However, with greater and greater frequency, managers are being asked to manage over long-distances using electronic media. This portion of the book focuses on how to perform distance coaching.

It is estimated by the International Telework Association and Council that there are over 23 million employees in the United States who work remotely at least part of the time. These employees are found in essentially every U.S. employment sector, but particularly in the manufacturing, business services, construction, banking, insurance, transport, and communications industries.

Extended business travel is at an all-time high. More and more employees are spending a substantial amount of their work hours at client sites, satellite offices, or home.

When an employee is working from a remote location, clear, regular, and defined coaching can be imperative to support the employee's professional effectiveness and growth.

Guidelines for Distance Coaching

It can be easy to forget about the developmental needs of an employee working away from the main office. And it is difficult to fully engage in coaching when you are not meeting face-to-face with an individual. Because of this, a manager needs to make an even *greater* effort to practice the five elements of *The Approach of a Coach* to succeed at distance coaching.

Let's revisit *The Approach of a Coach* in the context of distance coaching. Remember, a good coach:

1. Is deliberate and prepared.

2. Makes the coaching process mutual.

3. Strives to be a great communicator.

4. Is always looking for opportunities to coach.

5. Builds a coaching environment.

There are four main guidelines for fully engaging in *The Approach of a Coach* when coaching long distance. These are:

1. Make the most of different modes of communication.

2. Stay involved.

3. Keep the employee connected to the organization.

4. Clarify the structure for working long distance.

Make the Most of Different Modes of Communication

Today the options for electronic communication are many. They include individual telephone calls, telephone and video conferencing, groupware (computer technology for group communication), e-mail, and fax.

Use All Methods Available

It is important not to avoid phone calls simply because they take greater effort than e-mail. However, managers should not fall into the rut of just communicating via the phone or leaving phone messages. The effectiveness of a coaching call can be enhanced by supportive communication through other means. For example, an e-mail with detailed information or direction might be followed up with a clarifying phone call.

A manager can assess an employee in action by listening in on a conference call with a client or potential customer. Ongoing work can be monitored by requesting e-mail attachments or copies of work-related e-mails.

Leave Succinct Messages

When you spend time thinking through your message, you are more likely to leave one that is clear, effective, and succinct. If you leave an overly long voice mail message, you run the risk of it being deleted before all the information is received. The same thing can happen if you write an overly long e-mail.

Reiterate Important Points in Writing (Fax or E-mail)

The agenda for a coaching call can be faxed or e-mailed prior to the call and modified by both parties. After a phone call, e-mail or fax a summary of what you spoke about to encourage follow through.

➥ Case Example

Via e-mail, Katrina Stort, Sales Manager for a beverage supply company, wrote a succinct e-mail to her employee Jamal Wilson saying that she wanted to have a coaching session over the phone some time in the next week. Jamal was getting established in a new sales territory and Katrina wanted to clarify his short-term goals.

Once they agreed on a time, Katrina sent Jamal a copy of the things she wanted to discuss when they spoke and asked him for his feedback on the agenda. Katrina also faxed Jamal suggested guidelines for developing new customers from a company publication.

After their successful coaching call, Katrina e-mailed a summary of the main points they had discussed. Jamal regularly e-mailed to Katrina his completed weekly sales output summarized on a checklist they had developed during the meeting. They also interacted in the weekly staff meetings via telephone conferencing.

♦ ♦ ♦ ♦ ♦ ♦ ♦

Stay Involved

Plan how you are going to stay connected with the employee. Be as committed to the out-of-sight employee's professional needs as to the employee sitting in the next office.

Schedule Regular Telephone Calls

At the end of each call, set up the next one or establish a regular time of the week for a telephone meeting. This creates a sense of continuity and affiliation. It shows the employee that he or she is important and his or her job is important.

Schedule Occasional Face-to-Face Meetings

Even when you are diligent in using all the electronic means of communication available, occasionally meeting face-to-face with the employee is essential. It reinforces your relationship and enhances communication. If the employee does not regularly come to the main office, visit the employee at his or her work site. This will give you first-hand information and a chance to see and feel his or her working environment.

Specify How You Will Be Accessible

When an employee is working in the field or at home, he or she can feel isolated and disconnected. You are an important link to the organization for the employee. Make sure you are clear when and how the employee can contact you. Be prompt in your response.

➡ Case Example

Daryl Peters, Documents Management Manager for a large manufacturing company, supervises an off-site team that investigates and updates financial documents. He contacts Heather Lansbury, the Team Leader, twice a week by phone to discuss how she is overseeing the team and speaks with each member of the team every two weeks. He visits their operation quarterly.

Daryl has an "open door policy" and all of the employees on the team are invited to contact him with any issue. He has let it be known that he prefers an initial contact by e-mail and then schedules a call if necessary. He always promptly responds to e-mails or phone calls. He notifies the team whenever he will be unavailable for any extended amount of time.

◆ ◆ ◆ ◆ ◆ ◆ ◆

Keep the Employee Connected to the Organization

A good coach keeps employees aligned with the values and goals of the organization. The coach becomes a significant liaison between the distance worker and the organizational culture.

Share Information about the Organization and the Team

Make sure the employee receives up-to-date information about changes in organizational policy and structure. Register the distance worker on appropriate list servers or e-mail alerts.

Encourage Ongoing Contact between Team Members

Another way to keep the employee in touch with the organization is to suggest that distance workers maintain regular contact with other team members. Include all distance workers in staff meetings via telephone or video conferencing. Promote employee-to-employee contact in team meetings. Invite team members to use peer coaching as a tool for performance improvement.

➥ Case Example

Veteran Media Relations Specialist Lucinda Rolando recently began working from home after relocating out of state. Her boss, Lionel Wilbur, made sure that she was fully outfitted with all the necessary equipment to work long distance. He also set up a virtual private network via the Internet so that Lucinda could still access all the team files.

He asked Lucinda to teleconference into all the team meetings. However, on a number of occasions, her co-workers forgot to tell her about meetings that related to her work. This caused some confusion and hard feelings. At the next staff meeting, Lionel stressed the importance of remembering to keep Lucinda fully informed and encouraged all employees to "cc" Lucinda about anything related to her projects. He suggested that a new employee seek out some peer coaching with Lucinda concerning office operations.

♦ ♦ ♦ ♦ ♦ ♦ ♦

Clarify the Structure for Working Long Distance

Help Employees Establish an Effective Work Routine

When working outside the regular office, employees will benefit from setting up a clearly defined work environment wherever they are. It can be difficult to remain focused and efficient without the structure of the main office. Whether it's working from a hotel room, a home, a client site, or a satellite office, a coach can help employees organize their surroundings to fully support the work process.

The main point is for the distance worker to make a daily schedule and stick to it. The second point is to keep clear boundaries between work and other aspects of his or her life.

Agree upon How You Will Communicate

Try to establish agreements about how you will communicate with each other by asking questions like:

❖ "Do you prefer phone contact at the beginning or the end of the week?"

❖ "Do you like to talk in the morning or the evening?"

❖ "Would you rather communicate via e-mail and save phone calls for significant issues or do you prefer more frequent phone calling?"

➡ Case Example

Tina Bryslowski was annoyed. Home-based employee Jake Stewart sent five or six e-mails every day. Tina already had dozens of e-mails to go through daily. Because most of Jake's messages were inconsequential, Tina fell into the habit of only skimming through the messages and consequently missed an important fact about a reduction in product inventory. Tina also noticed that the e-mails were generally written late at night and was concerned about the regularity of Jake's work habits.

Tina sent Jake an e-mail requesting a coaching phone call. She stated that in the phone meeting she'd like to review the process of how they communicated as well as discuss Jake's daily routine. She made sure that she wrote this message in a non-threatening way.

During the phone call, Tina asked Jake to think about which topics did or did not need to be communicated to Tina. They agreed that Jake would make a list of different subject areas and prioritize them to be discussed in the next coaching call.

They also discussed Jake's work routine to find out if he was setting clear boundaries between work and home life. Tina suggested a time management course to help Jake better plan his schedule to help with his focus and efficiency.

◆ ◆ ◆ ◆ ◆ ◆ ◆

Using Long-Distance Communication Media

The three most common long-distance coaching media include:

1. Coaching telephone calls.

2. Coaching e-mails.

3. Coaching conference calls via phone or video.

Coaching Telephone Calls

Several factors make a coaching telephone call successful. They are:

1. Structuring the call.

2. Paying particular attention to the paralinguistics of the speaker's voice.

3. Checking out reactions frequently.

Structuring the Call

It's easy to be too casual on the telephone. Prepare the same way you would a face-to-face coaching session. Be clear about the purpose of the telephone call. For instance, you might say, "I wanted to hear about what you've been doing and how I can be of help. Give me a summary of your day and then tell me specifics of what is giving you a tough time."

Paying Attention to the Paralinguistics of the Speaker's Voice

Paralinguistics have to do with the tone, volume, and inflection of a person's voice. Since you are losing the other nonverbal information available when coaching in-person, the paralinguistic qualities of the employee take on even more importance. For example, does the employee's voice sound stressed, disturbed, or agitated? Is the employee quieter than usual or more hesitant? Follow up these observations with active inquiry to understand what the other person is experiencing or trying to communicate.

Checking Out Reactions Frequently

Touch base regularly with the employee. Ask about their reactions to what is being discussed and if the conversation is helpful. Do everything you can to avoid miscommunication. For example, you can regularly ask questions like, "Does this make sense?" or "What do you think about that?"

Coaching E-mails

E-mails are very convenient, but they can also be a dangerous mode of business communication. Unless used with care and sensitivity, they can easily become a fertile ground for growing misperceptions and false assumptions. Most people do not put the same effort into an e-mail as they would a letter. The ease of response makes it very easy to respond prematurely or inappropriately. The communication of information without emotional content can often lead to negative conclusions.

Vault.com, a workplace research firm, conducted a survey of 1,000 workers. They found that 51 percent of respondents said that the tone of their e-mails is often misperceived. The misperceptions include viewing the e-mail as angry, too casual, or abrupt.

Consequently, when adopting a coaching focus with an e-mail, a coach needs to take extra care to communicate with clarity. If some sort of tension develops around what has been said in an e-mail, make a telephone call or meet in-person to clarify the true message that was intended.

Here are five points to remember when sending coaching e-mails:

1. Take time when writing your e-mail.
2. Clearly state the purpose of the e-mail.
3. Make an extra effort to add positive feedback.
4. Review your e-mail twice before sending it.
5. Make sure your e-mails have been received.

Take Time When Writing Your E-mail

Do not rush! Give some deliberate thought to what you want to communicate. Add language that communicates emotion to clarify the framework of your message.

Clearly State the Purpose of the E-mail

Try to avoid ambiguous e-mails. We may be clear about the reason for the e-mail, but the recipient needs to have the framework spelled out.

Make an Extra Effort to Add Positive Feedback

You can use an e-mail as an opportunity to reinforce something the employee has done well. At the same time, you create a positive tone to the e-mail.

Review Your E-mail Twice before Sending

Check for typing and grammatical errors. Errors suggest you don't think the employee is important enough for you to make an effort. Make sure the content is personable and understandable. Think how the recipient will view what's written.

Make Sure E-mails Have Been Received

Many e-mail server software programs now have the capability to ask for confirmation of receipt of a sent e-mail. If not, reference the e-mail in your next communication to the employee to make sure it was received.

➥ Case Example

Here is an example of both a poorly written e-mail and an effective one.

> Burt,
>
> Get me an update on the Lovitt Company project as soon as possible. I was expecting it earlier.
>
> Abe

* *

> Burt,
>
> Thanks for the great work you've been doing coordinating the administration of the Stilwood project. I specifically liked the way you spelled out the reasons for the change to the completion date.
>
> As we spoke about in our last coaching call, you were going to update me about the Lovitt Company project. I was hoping to receive your update by today so I could review it prior to our call on Thursday. I know things have been hectic for you, but I want to make sure we stay on track with the customer service improvement goals we set last time we spoke.
>
> Thanks,
> Abe

◆ ◆ ◆ ◆ ◆ ◆ ◆

Coaching Conference Calls

Another form of long-distance coaching is the coaching conference call in which a number of employees meet over the telephone or via video.

The same rules apply as with team coaching. In a conference call, you can use the structure for effective meetings described on page 105. Have the agenda sent to everyone well before the start of the meeting. If available, use computer groupware to keep track of agenda items and action planning during the meeting. Remember to follow up by sending any important decisions and action points via e-mail or fax.

In conference call coaching, there is an even greater need to pay attention to the process of the meeting and to facilitate participation and clarification of obstacles. For a conference call to be most effective, the coach needs to be an assertive facilitator. Without assertive facilitation, a conference call can easily degenerate into a meandering, confused, or contentious meeting.

Here are five elements to effectively facilitate a coaching conference call:

1. Pause routinely to create space for comments.

2. Regularly ask for feedback.

3. Have go-rounds where every person comments about the topic.

4. Specifically ask for comments from quiet employees.

5. Keep notes to stay on top of what has been said.

Pause Routinely to Create Space for Comments

Be silent for a time. It will encourage others to talk. A pause also gives people time to digest what has been discussed.

Regularly Ask for Feedback

Directly ask how people think and feel about the topic. Ask if the meeting is on track.

Have Go-Rounds in Which Every Person Comments about the Topic

Take each person's "temperature" about what is being discussed. Make sure each person gets to speak without interruption. After everyone has spoken, summarize what has been said.

Specifically Ask for Comments from Quiet Employees

It's easy to forget about someone who hasn't been speaking. Keep track of participation and involve those who haven't contributed.

Keep Notes to Stay on Top of What Has Been Said

Jot down important comments and decisions. Keep track of action points. Make notes to yourself about the process of the meeting.

Let's review.

The four main guidelines for **distance coaching** are:

❖ **Make the most of different modes of communication**

❖ **Stay involved**

❖ **Keep the employee connected to the organization**

❖ **Clarify the structure for working long distance**

There are a variety of factors to remember when using long-distance media for coaching.

When making **coaching telephone calls:**

❖ **Structure the call**

❖ **Pay particular attention to the paralinguistics of the speaker's voice**

❖ **Check out reactions frequently**

When writing **coaching e-mails:**

❖ **Take time when writing your e-mail**

❖ **Clearly state the purpose of the e-mail**

❖ **Make an extra effort to add positive feedback**

❖ **Review your e-mail twice before sending it**

❖ **Make sure your e-mails have been received**

When making **coaching conference calls:**

❖ **Pause routinely to create space for comments**

❖ **Regularly ask for feedback**

❖ **Have go-rounds where every person comments about the topic**

❖ **Specifically ask for comments from quiet employees**

❖ **Keep notes to stay on top of what has been said**

Epilogue

Most employees want to do their best at work. However, the road to workplace success can be challenging and complicated. Coaching an employee through the process can be extremely beneficial. A supportive coach can make the difference between success and failure.

The manager's role as a coach is one of the most important and rewarding aspects of a manager's job. Coaching employees to develop their skills helps not only the employee, but also the manager, the team, and the organization.

About the Author

Dr. Daniel Feldman, President of Leadership Performance Solutions of Falls Church, Virginia, is a consulting psychologist who has worked with corporate, government, and nonprofit organizations for over 20 years.

Dr. Feldman helps organizations improve their effectiveness through leadership development, process facilitation, and team building and has designed and facilitated a wide variety of human capital development programs. In his role as an executive coach and master facilitator, Dr. Feldman has the ability to give a depth of understanding to the essential skills for workplace success.

Dr. Feldman is the author of *The Handbook of Emotionally Intelligent Leadership* and a frequent speaker on the topics of leadership, emotional intelligence, and coaching. Dr. Feldman received his Doctorate in Counseling Psychology from Virginia Commonwealth University.

Index